One thousand thoughts

In five words or less

John Chaffee

 DRIFTING SPIRIT SONGS, LLC™

From "*The Pledge of Allegiance*," originally conceived by Captain George Thatcher Balch. Formally adopted by Congress in 1942 and officially named in 1945.

WHY FIVE WORDS OR LESS?

I woke up one morning with the words "to like, to want, is" in my head. I don't know where the phrase came from or why it was there, but I wrote it down. And then other thoughts came and I wrote them down. And after twenty or so, I noticed they were all five words or less. You'd be surprised at what you can express with such an economy of words: "I will love you forever." "One nation, under God, indivisible." "Cement leads a hard life." I kept going and now, here they are – one thousand thoughts in five words or less. Some are whimsical, some are profound, some are heartfelt, some are pure nonsense and some may stir deep emotion. Some you may have even said yourself more than once without realizing they're five words or less. Oh, and if a thousand isn't enough, I've left some blank pages at the end of the book for you to include your own thoughts, in five words or less ... "think about it, won't you?"

——— JC

Five words or more

from award-winning author Howard Giordano:

"So, John, I read them all, and as I said in my 'first glance' reaction to the first few pages: some are meaningless, some rang true, and some … wow! I started to list my favorites from each page but stopped a few pages in. After looking them over, I realized that my selections say an awful lot about who I am – or at least, *who I think I am*. It's a pretty telling exercise."

Howard's books, *The Second Target* and *Tracking Terror*, are available at Amazon.com.

The thoughts ...

1

To like, to want, is

2

Burn your demons

3

Maybe someday comes

4

Sorry, there's no explanation

5

Embrace your spirit

6

Be kind and true

7

Somersaults are for the young

8

This time matters

9

Legs fold, arms hold

10

Even people lay an egg

11
There will always be forever

12
There once was a memory

13
Get out of your cradle

14
Carve your life cleanly

15
Somewhere there's a twin

16
Don't live under water

17
Far away, a light

18
When it calls, answer

19
Look, obstacles aren't really there

20
Silliness leads to laughter

21

Principles are principal

22

Too much is not enough

23

Trust takes care of things

24

Shade windows to the soul

25

Curmudgeons are people, too

26

Everyone sings, joy it brings

27

Ancestors, alive in our hearts

28

Wyoming, in a quiet state

29

Speak in earth tones

30

Look for rainbows, not gold

31
Chairs should be momentary

32
A twig cannot trip you

33
Wild animals are better wild

34
Faraway loves are always close

35
Dreams come to those awake

36
Rifts in family are preventable

37
Some roots, buried, are invisible

38
There'll never be another now

39
Wind, a friend, an enemy

40
Go sit in the park

41

Go stand on your own

42

What is that baby thinking

43

All nights aren't dark

44

Start a conversation, make friends

45

If trouble comes, sing

46

A smile is a welcome

47

Take advantage of the morning

48

A friend is a gift

49

Work to have fun

50

There is always time

51

Don't say maybe, say yes

52

Keep your friends real close

53

The summer is never over

54

Life doesn't have to decay

55

You can fly, try

56

There's no reason to quit

57

Fear not, it won't happen

58

March out of step

59

Possibilities should always be awake

60

Eat up food for thought

61

Ashes are signs of life

62

Bear your cross humbly

63

Go get going now

64

Remember to forget yesterday

65

Struggle until the next one

66

I believe, yes I do

67

Forgiveness is habit forming

68

Jump higher than you can

69

Don't keep saying don't, do

70

From life's ropes, break free

71
Strangers can be friends

72
Your dog knows your name

73
Sometimes the answer is obscured

74
Look around, life is there

75
Every chance you get, take

76
Ouch is a warning cry

77
Escalators, life's ups and downs

78
Speed limits, limits on speed

79
The sky has no limit

80
Our planet is a miracle

81
Sleep in your own bed

82
Are left-handers usually right

83
Even winding roads straighten out

84
When you're lost, ask

85
Always say yes to challenges

86
Pick a place and go

87
Pick a pace and go

88
Show a child yourself

89
See more when you explore

90
We go, our memories stay

91
Try not to disappoint yourself

92
Like to listen to yourself

93
The ugliest animal isn't ugly

94
No caution, stop, or go

95
Always check your messages

96
Clouds eventually lift

97
Careful picking up broken glass

98
Have some variety, mix well

99
It's what's behind your eyes

100
Ignore all things sterile

101

Don't mimic the mediocre

102

Be proud of your reflection

103

Put others before selfie

104

Love's not a passing emotion

105

Learn everything you can

106

Teach everything you can

107

Mingle with the best

108

Success comes after doubt goes

109

Hey, how are you doing

110

Life is uphill, breathe deeply

111
Integrity, not for sale

112
Don't betray your conscience

113
Think of your words first

114
I will love you forever

115
Don't be a bad person

116
You can't save the world

117
Make sure your shoes fit

118
Your neighbor appreciates your help

119
Elvis' voice did not die

120
Hugs, bandages for the brain

121

The mirror sees you naked

122

Deep down, they love you

123

Get under a banana's skin

124

Take yourself lightly, others do

125

Go for it, it beckons

126

Listen for the starter's gun

127

Spare me, spare ribs, too

128

The magic is in you

129

Amateurs do beat professionals

130

Have you had yours lately?

131
Celebrate your birthday with style

132
Sometimes I deserved a spanking

133
Now and then, giggle

134
Take your wet clothes off

135
Make my fries crispy

136
The world isn't your oyster

137
A starry night is heaven

138
Walk, run, drive, act, safely

139
Bring joy to the world

140
Try not to fall, much

141
What is it you want

142
I can't help it mom

143
Nothing is beyond repair

144
Celebrate the lessons in life

145
Be an ocean, make waves

146
It's all worth the pain

147
Surrender shouldn't be an action

148
Practice doesn't always make perfect

149
Read a lot of books

150
Look nice for loved ones

151
You can't take back lies

152
Thinking too much is exhausting

153
Be what makes you happy

154
A smile melts a heart

155
It helps to apologize

156
There's no pill for success

157
Politicians are great dancers

158
Only one stupid question allowed

159
Retirement is just one step

160
Always dress to suit yourself

161
If you wait you'll miss

162
Don't be late for life

163
Drugs do good, and don't

164
Only smoke if on fire

165
Does anyone really know you

166
Talk more than you text

167
Clear time to do nothing

168
Help yourself to happiness

169
I'm not crazy, are you

170
Tall, tell, till, toll, tulle

171
No hill is insurmountable

172
Of course there's an answer

173
A good walk clears cobwebs

174
Shine your light on all

175
Stay away from bad influences

176
Don't hide your emotions

177
Sad moments are just moments

178
Carnival rides free your spirit

179
How many decibels are necessary

180
Always enjoy life's frills

181

Anyone can become a legend

182

Always heed any alarm

183

There's always a way out

184

Let's count all our blessings

185

Compliments cost nothing to give

186

Remember, gravity is the law

187

Keep a parachute handy

188

Give the best gift, yourself

189

Perseverance cannot be stopped

190

Be someone's biggest fan

191
Don't forget to say thanks

192
Be like the sun, shine

193
Winning is no accident

194
People love a care package

195
Be prepared to stop

196
Obey the law, or else

197
Doing favors is a stimulant

198
Erase your negativity permanently

199
You can feel your ghosts

200
Take a holiday from stress

201
Winners think differently

202
Always run toward things

203
Be open to surprise

204
Keep your heart's door unlocked

205
Children love a good teacher

206
No battle is easily won

207
Have faith in yourself first

208
A roadblock is only temporary

209
Happened yesterday and that's gone

210
Head for new frontiers

211

Compliments are hearing aids

212

Try to sleep counting friends

213

There's peace in the woods

214

Is that picture really you?

215

Are you a love graduate?

216

Judges sometimes make bad judgments

217

Shouldn't everyone keep a diary

218

Have you ever thanked yourself?

219

What's an antisocial network?

220

Where is your role model?

221

'Til death do us part

222

Do it for the team

223

Shazam is for the gods

224

Don't forget, government is you

225

Out west they still do

226

Stand apart from the crowd

227

Be not ashamed or repentant

228

In all situations, act accordingly

229

The moon is always full

230

Always remember, you're an entertainer

231
You'll never forget your first

232
Families are built on love

233
Don't ever cross that line

234
What are you afraid of

235
Aim for the small circle

236
Always play by the rules

237
Tomorrow will come soon enough

238
Thin skin causes fat lips

239
Pencils write pointed questions

240
Expel germs of all kinds

241

Aren't we moving too fast

242

Good deeds are rewarded

243

Nightmares end in a flash

244

Build a strong self

245

Broken relationships can be rebuilt

246

Broken promises won't be forgotten

247

Cement lives a hard life

248

Honor and courage define you

249

Paleontologists are yesterday's news

250

Don't give up your rights

251

Copycats are never first

252

Obey your doctor's orders

253

Believe in your higher power

254

Compete equally, complete individually

255

Pause on the high wire

256

We are all storytellers

257

A rolling stone travels downward

258

Never quiet never bored

259

We're only guests here

260

Losing weight, don't wait

261

God bless you, America, too

262

You're cleared for takeoff

263

You can't succeed part time

264

All are created equal

265

Your barber can be trusted

266

Liberty and justice for all*

267

Where will you go next

268

Even Superman had a weakness

269

Wait, don't take the bait

270

Time is best spent giving

271
Even turtles eventually get there.

272
Your world is always spinning

273
People change, but not much

274
Do you remember your birthday

275
Are there pills for everything

276
Mummies, wrapped up in themselves

277
Read a book, transport yourself

278
Lose yourself in yourself

279
Reach out and touch

280
The simple things are not

281
Walk all over the place

282
Technology is cool, not warm

283
The journey is always interesting

284
Guess who I am today

285
I've always loved a mystery

286
Shackles are for the uninspired

287
Your troubles will be mine

288
Try to remember the good

289
Time flies, use it wisely

290
Funnel cakes are good food

291
Do better than your best

292
Act crazy now and then

293
Make your bed every day

294
Always fly under the radar

295
Don't let the barnacles attach

296
Whatever gave me this idea

297
There is beauty in all

298
Country roads lead to peace

299
Be little, don't belittle

300
Pressure opens the thinking pores

301

That song is always there

302

Home is where you belong

303

And then, it was quiet

304

Was the joke on me

305

Tears of joy are better

306

Protect and project your spine

307

You are a superhero if

308

Adventures are around every corner

309

Use caution changing your mind

310

One nation, under God, indivisible*

311
Get ready, raise the bar

312
I'm not available right now

313
Please signal before you turn

314
Stay off the beaten path

315
What would I do, without

316
You have to be fast

317
I am who I am

318
Stay in your own lane

319
Little sisters sometimes protect you

320
Stop signs mean just that

321
For the love of God

322
Cover your ears when snooping

323
There are things called miracles

324
Stay away from shallow people

325
Mince is not a meat

326
Good service should be automatic

327
Spread your wings wider, wider

328
Keep your mind in motion

329
There is no free lunch

330
Might does not make right

331
Walk miles in their shoes

332
Be firm in your beliefs

333
No excuses are good excuses

334
Bare trees signify gloomy days

335
A barn's inside's always alive

336
Enjoy a slice of watermelon

337
I can't, is not acceptable

338
Pledge allegiance to the flag*

339
Enjoy, don't cause, fireworks

340
Big families have less room

341
Hard work never killed anybody

342
Thomas Edison lit the way

343
Remember, you are an animal

344
Ask a stranger to dance

345
Don't buy time, it's free

346
We are all temporarily able

347
Walls are for climbing over

348
Pretend you're in the circus

349
I stake my reputation on

350
Won't you stand by me

351
Someone is missing at Christmas

352
Don't leave it to fate

353
Don't play poker without bluffing

354
Get a good night's sleep

355
Enjoy life in slower traffic

356
Go find roses to smell

357
Climate changes indoors, too

358
Store your phone at dinner

359
Fields get plowed, you shouldn't

360
Stay out of the swamp

361

It's all downhill on snowboards

362

Don't name your boy Sue

363

Porcupines are not for cuddling

364

Stay zipped up in public

365

Be courageous, fight authority

366

Of course Bigfoot exists, right?

367

Clean up all your messes

368

When wrong, hit the brakes

369

The best donation is you

370

Be your own pilot

371
Be careful on icy paths

372
Leave the guard rails alone

373
Try the other side sometime

374
Can weeping willows be happy

375
Go ahead, start something

376
May your days be merry

377
Potty trained, not potty mouth

378
Imagine you're in heaven

379
Money can buy some happiness

380
I know where Waldo is

381
Trucks can carry the weight

382
Infinity, a long time coming

383
Can crooked people straighten out

384
Don't talk dirty too often

385
The fog will lift, eventually

386
Home runs are for everyone

387
Charity begins at your home

388
Read the Bill of Rights

389
You can know the unknown

390
Patience and tolerance are golden

391
Do what you do best

392
You have to earn wings

393
Stay on the right track

394
In glass houses, wear clothes

395
Will I see you again

396
Give me your password

397
If you can't swim, wade

398
Get off at Exit One

399
Watch for slow merging people

400
One dollar buys not much

401
A thank you is therapeutic

402
Charge your battery regularly

403
We live on borrowed time

404
There's no substitute for love

405
No one is almost naked

406
Feeling bad? Go shop awhile

407
Why not dessert first

408
Mom always liked me best

409
Mother's day is every day

410
Needles get under your skin

411

Are you sure of yourself

412

Healthy people are happy people

413

Wander wisely, then come home

414

Be careful who you engage

415

I ate the whole thing

416

Strength and gentleness are compatible

417

Be generous with your praise

418

Do not curb your enthusiasm

419

Bad behavior shouldn't be excused

420

That's for the birds

421
Lay parallel with the universe

422
Why is hair so important

423
Order your life well done

424
Be sharp isn't a note

425
Profanity is always dirty

426
Laughter is real good medicine

427
Recycle the good things

428
Sometimes the world acts drunk

429
Curiosity kills cats, not me

430
Grab mornings by the grits

431
If you study, you're smart

432
Grow at your own pace

433
Love one another with heart

434
Don't talk trash, toss it

435
Decide which records you want

436
Learn lessons from the past

437
Try, try and try again

438
Finish what's on your plate

439
Every word you say counts

440
Marry someone you put first

441
Break out of your slump

442
You don't have to quit

443
Enjoy the sound of music

444
Know you are a star

445
The mailbox always has surprises

446
Keep moving when near vultures

447
Pay attention to your conscience

448
Gamblers take a big chance

449
When opportunity calls, answer it

450
Trouble is always moments away

451
Answer all cries for help

452
Time heals most wounds

453
Most of all, be you

454
Don't give up the ship

455
Veterinarians go to the dogs

456
Marijuana won't make you faster

457
Always wear clean underwear

458
Hard to swallow soft drinks

459
Hold your head up high

460
Seek a level playing field

461
Your opinion is never wrong

462
Crotchety people lose friends

463
Love only works if shared

464
Children playing are life's treasures

465
Are you passenger or pilot

466
Keep baggage to a minimum

467
Families work better together

468
Ask for more than needed

469
What's the most meaningful gift

470
Your valuables are only things

471
Make something out of nothing

472
Listen for life's special moments

473
Long ago and far away

474
Earth takes care of itself

475
How does your garden grow

476
Don't waver, waffle or washout

477
Only you limit your potential

478
Look for the heaviest weight

479
Sometimes don't act your age

480
Be honest with yourself, too

481
Defeat is something to avoid

482
Drinking lawyers try many cases

483
Be aware of every exit

484
Crushes are sometimes crushed

485
You are also a satellite

486
Which version of you matters

487
Tell me about your past

488
Some things aren't hands free

489
Some answers are still missing

490
Impossible dreams may not be

491
People can't get factory resets

492
Things change in a blink

493
You're always on candid camera

494
The basics are most important

495
People like seeing thumbs up

496
Your seat's reserved in heaven

497
Wake up before the roosters

498
Be a good sport always

499
Keep your distance from hate

500
We are all jugglers

501
Pay your bills on time

502
Political correctness is an oxymoron

503
Write an unauthorized autobiography

504
Rest if you get tired

505
Very nice to meet you

506
Proud to have served you

507
Easy to forget the ordinary

508
Always be the best prepared

509
Patience, pluck, perseverance,
partnership, promotion

510
Life is simple, not easy

511
Find an age specific playground

512
Always lend a helping hand

513
Show everyone the real you

514
Dig deep when adversity strikes

515
Flat-Earthers are 'round here

516
Don't stop thinking of others

517
Negative thoughts will come true

518
When feeling down, look up

519
Both feet on the ground

520
If you could live forever

521
Should life be a mystery

522
Will you accept someone unusual

523
Looking for a good sport

524
Should not be hyphenated Americans

525
Clowns will change your mood

526
Mom says eat your vegetables

527
Make no mistake about it

528
Obey your wake-up call

529
Put your gum somewhere else

530
No hill for high steppers

531
Waste not, want not

532
Come in from the cold

533
Barbers specialize in close shaves

534
OK now, what's next

535
Put your mask away

536
Does life owe you anything

537
Even small miracles are big

538
The best do not rest

539
There is no easy way

540
Is love really a battlefield

541
Not tired, but sleeping together

542
Words will never hurt me

543
Don't ever sell your soul

544
Your church is within you

545
Try not to skip school

546
Be firm when stalking stability

547
This is no laughing matter

548
Oh sweet smell of victory

549
Mosquitos all have blood relatives

550
You don't have to go

551
Offense is the best defense

552
Music is the universal language

553
All we want is love

554
Be anything but ordinary

555
Stay away from foul play

556
The Lord is my shepherd

557
Drive a car that's you

558
Will I be OK

559
Flowers are gifts of life

560
Just say it out loud

561
Just laugh over spilt milk

562
Everyone's put out to pasture

563
Who sings the last song

564
Let misery love another's company

565
Leave your nest while young

566
Stand up for your rights

567
Anyone can lift a dumbbell

568
Exploit the craft you've mastered

569
You won't win the lottery

570
Why don't you try harder

571
One step at a time

572
Happiness is your own making

573
Just going about my business

574
I know how to play

575
Cleanliness is next to impossible

576
Only one chance at life

577
Don't jump into the mainstream

578
Driver's training doesn't always work

579
Get off my property now

580
Do you smell something fishy

581

You can't teach motivation

582

Ain't is not ain't it

583

Too broke to pay attention

584

Please return your shopping cart

585

We are all eventually handicapped

586

Would Einstein understand new math

587

Losing is part of life

588

I will always be true

589

If easy, it's not worthwhile

590

Work and play aren't incompatible

591
I don't think I'm weird

592
Plant some seeds today

593
There is no harmless word

594
Make a long story short

595
Sleeping is undercover work

596
Is it better to go

597
Look around and see more

598
Half empty is half full

599
Don't miss a starry night

600
You make problems go away

601
Let your best friend know

602
Give your life story life

603
Sad days are always longer

604
What one thing defines you

605
No one succeeds by oneself

606
How large is your universe

607
Never paint your screen door

608
Don't take candy from babies

609
Always extend your abilities

610
You shouldn't fool yourself

611

Lobsters can get boiling mad

612

People die, deeds live on

613

School isn't for the disinterested

614

The meek won't inherit much

615

Paint your life without pastels

616

Practice the horn of plenty

617

Make believe makes life fun

618

Some mysteries can't be solved

619

Imagine, believe, imagine, believe, do

620

Are you pawn or knight

621
Maybe isn't a good answer

622
Don't ever forget a playground

623
Watch intently for good vibrations

624
Be ready willing and able

625
Cheering for your team excites

626
Don't let yourself dinosaur think

627
Chocolate must come from heaven

628
When in danger call Batman

629
Write letters now and then

630
Build don't burn bridges

631

Jogging your memory is healthy

632

Don't say I don't care

633

Magic isn't just for magicians

634

I'm not my mother yet

635

Care to be carefree

636

Make your own breeze

637

What is your life song

638

Get it off your mind

639

Actions speak louder than silence

640

Don't follow, be the leader

641
My friends are the best

642
Keep making good memories

643
It's easy to hate hate

644
Name a drug that heals

645
How many friendships will last

646
To ponder is to wonder

647
You can trust shady trees

648
You can fix flat tires

649
You can't fix stupid

650
We all need play time

651
What takes your breath away

652
Live in the fast lane

653
Even older respect your elders

654
Will a wallflower grow

655
Shake things up for once

656
Each one of us climbs

657
Crazy in love isn't crazy

658
Can't drink at bar none

659
Pets will make you happy

660
Come to my emotional rescue

661

Home exists in the heart

662

Plagiarism is for copycats

663

Absence makes the heart drift

664

Doing little is doing nothing

665

Love is not for sissies

666

Aspirin won't relieve a heartache

667

Fraudulent people lie with ease

668

Hands in pockets don't work

669

Sage advice is no herb

670

Placebos are nothing to me

671
Liars lips move the same

672
What cartoon character are you

673
Voodoo dolls are for professionals

674
Are you settling for okay

675
How much can you take

676
Do you need a lawyer

677
Small minds can't travel far

678
What are you waiting for

679
The cave man never texted

680
Are men working signs sexist

681
Dance like there's no tomorrow

682
Politicians speak with forked tongues

683
Caramelizing is a sticky subject

684
Face time is valuable time

685
Don't apologize when right

686
So you think you're clever

687
The drinks are on you

688
Tomorrow will come soon enough

689
Are you sensitive to nuts

690
Don't ever lose your marbles

691
Think out loud and pray

692
Life is full of surprises

693
Do not run with scissors

694
Recycle your worries and fears

695
You can stumble, don't fall

696
Teachers only teach the willing

697
Where there's smoke there's intrigue

698
Is God in your family

699
All gamblers eventually lose

700
Life can be a dream

701
Don't start a monkey business

702
Are you on the level

703
Who's your next door neighbor

704
Always be prepared for battle

705
Allow yourself to be naked

706
When you juggle don't miss

707
You're on stage, act well

708
Isn't it fun being childish

709
When your soul trembles, laugh

710
The jungle is not safe

711
Veterans served and now deserve

712
Fireflies light the night free

713
Juxtapose the words give I

714
What are you living for

715
Cowboys horse around sometimes

716
We're all here to entertain

717
We're all here to serve

718
The moon is always full

719
Mark my words you say

720
Every day do something amazing

721
Automobiles are transportation not weapons

722
There's only one Mother Earth

723
Drink in moderation when possible

724
We can't let cancer win

725
The world needs positive thinkers

726
Don't ever act your age

727
Save more than a penny

728
Faster service at the window

729
Runners don't need athlete's foot

730
Don't play games with me

731
What makes you crazy

732
Awesome are eagles in flight

733
Continue having birthday parties

734
What danger drives you

735
Shed only tears of joy

736
You're always in a parade

737
Unsolved mysteries can be solved

738
No one is accident free

739
You can't change your personality

740
Snow is not always welcome

741
When opportunity knocks, answer

742
Try not to make enemies

743
Surprise someone with a card

744
Be your own biggest fan

745
Yes I can do this

746
Mountains exist for climbers

747
Turn on a love light

748
Please give me a cookie

749
Go ahead, wiggle your butt

750
There is only this moment

751
Smiles can wipe out darkness

752
A child's laugh can heal

753
Is it worth fighting for

754
After all, it's just a game

755
Which way should I go

756
Why don't you call them

757
My dog is gone, doggone

758
Mindless acts are missing something

759
Lend, or give, a hand

760
Toss, don't hold, a grudge

761
Why don't you believe me

762
Break your own records

763
Live life with exclamation points

764
Have you hugged someone today

765
You're higher on cloud ten

766
Your presence is my present

767
Whatever you do, have fun

768
Something fishy about the water

769
Make your dreams come true

770
Don't leave the party early

771
Because I said so

772
I don't want an excuse

773
Always signal before you turn

774
Stick to it, use glue

775
Life ain't a spectator sport

776
Don't ever rumble with thunder

777
You sure are beautiful

778
Accept criticism but not easily

779
Don't go near the edge

780
You're sober, you drive home

781
Would you like to dance

782
No such thing as free

783
What gets you the highest

784
If only I owned that

785
When will you stop griping

786
Be honest with yourself

787
Build something that lasts

788
When driving yourself crazy, park

789
Nothing beats being well-balanced

790
Always fasten your seat belt

791
There is only one you

792
Sorry, you'll never find perfect

793
Love won't let you down

794
It's good to be different

795
Keep on trying to improve

796
The innocence of baby talk

797
Sunny days lift me up

798
A coat only covers something

799
What if I said no

800
What if I said yes

801

You deserve a quiet place

802

Alcohol can create the unexpected

803

What else don't you know

804

At a loss for words

805

Time doesn't march, it crawls

806

Above all else, persevere

807

What do you appreciate most

808

I'm living in surreal times

809

Fast is the new slow

810

These arms long for you

811

Time to wake up

812

Dance around a bit

813

Mothers are the best people

814

I'll never do that again

815

Always pack your own parachute

816

Autumn leaves, love stays

817

Words speak louder than anything

818

I might change the world

819

Stay away from gluttony

820

Pay your bills on time

821

Learn to accept others

822

There's no place like home

823

When riding high come down

824

You know who lacks brainpower

825

Plant the seeds of understanding

826

No good deed goes unnoticed

827

Remember where you came from

828

Lift somebody else's spirits

829

Always let the sunshine in

830

Nobody needs a bullhorn

831
Eating out's really eating in

832
Is there a last straw

833
Is this all there is

834
Think about your last meal

835
Are you a better parent

836
Glue won't repair broken promises

837
Don't out-clever yourself

838
Tell me that's not true

839
Like it or not, sushi

840
Irrelevance means nothing to me

841

I wish it were so

842

Are you proud of yourself

843

Have you tried again

844

The right words can heal

845

Who's your favorite friend

846

Can you change your mind

847

Only one thing lasts forever

848

No crime to kill time

849

Can you keep a secret

850

Shine a light on all

851
Pleasure seekers will find it

852
Traffic jam is not edible

853
Try hard, figure it out

854
Knock on wood softly

855
Why did I do that

856
Don't rely on strength alone

857
Concentrate on what you're doing

858
I can use your help

859
Then again I just might

860
Talk to yourself with prayer

861

Dawn doesn't break, it opens

862

That's too much to eat

863

What if there was peace

864

You can't drive me crazy

865

A child can lead you

866

Drink too much and fail

867

There's enough to go around

868

What does whip smart mean

869

First place is your destination

870

You can't stop forward progress

871
If you were a flower

872
Why not twitch your nose

873
When angry just forget why

874
You have something to give

875
Pretend it doesn't hurt

876
Go hunting for good things

877
Behave when out in public

878
A dreamer finds true love

879
Do things you won't regret

880
Better not let mom know

881

What is part and parcel

882

How do you feel now

883

I love to watch people

884

I like just desserts

885

Is anyone afraid of nothing

886

Always be a good sport

887

Life goes on and on

888

Is it gross or net

889

No thank you I'm driving

890

I'll get a birdie tomorrow

891
Nothing compares to plain spoken

892
Keep on learning your lessons

893
Always rest a spell

894
Pizza bakers have it made

895
Crushes can leave you crushed

896
Does anyone hear your secrets

897
Is your biggest fan overhead

898
Are some bad habits good

899
We play in one orchestra

900
How is anyone semi-anything

901
Little lies aren't really little

902
It's best to stay regular

903
Don't stray far from love

904
And I say why not

905
Please is a good word

906
Cookies make you feel better

907
America is beautiful beyond words

908
Then there's the party party

909
We can't agree on everything

910
If you drink don't sing

911
Sun doesn't set, earth rotates

912
Old people have golden arches

913
Don't let no stop you

914
How far is far out

915
Don't wait up for me

916
Doesn't matter where you're from

917
Preparing mentally for the game

918
Live love and laugh heartily

919
Less than five words

920
What's the difference anyway

921
Wake up as someone else

922
Don't hide under the covers

923
The common man, not uncommon

924
Buy a car that's you

925
Don't live in the dark

926
Running wild leaves you breathless

927
Keep your distance from sloth

928
Enjoy your time alone

929
Why don't you grow up

930
You did that on purpose

931
Fairy tales can come true

932
What's the definition of love

933
I think therefore you are

934
A handshake is a seal

935
How long can you go

936
Victories taste best when earned

937
Don't try to stop evolution

938
Slow down now and then

939
I'll try harder than you

940
Nothing gives pleasure like giving

941

Stay still during a blackout

942

Is there a silver opportunity

943

Help is on the way

944

Do chickens really cross roads

945

Always clean up after yourself

946

Perseverance brings rewards

947

Make a note of everything

948

We all have to lead

949

Light a fire in yourself

950

Exercise your brain, too

951
Luck comes to prepared minds

952
Love is not really blind

953
A patient with patience heals

954
Never ignore a beep

955
Courteous people are rewarded

956
What makes you say "ouch"

957
Faith is a great motivator

958
Pretend you didn't see that

959
Practice only the good things

960
A shrug isn't an answer

961
Litterbugs don't bite but hurt

962
Do people ever become antiques

963
Stamp collectors stick to it

964
Respect and honor the flag

965
Nothing is partly finished

966
It's time to speak up

967
You can't insult a fool

968
The decline of common language

969
Perform your duties with grace

970
How fast can you react

971

Thinking out loud might irritate

972

Throw away useless things

973

Don't let cloudy days discourage

974

Shutting down for a minute

975

You make my head spin

976

Play the sport of life

977

Always do the right thing

978

The hardest test is best

979

Go your own way first

980

Please please please clean up

981
You can't resist the munchies

982
School is with you forever

983
Treat yourself to new experiences

984
Football players tackle big problems

985
What does drink responsibly mean

986
Keep the end far away

987
Try, you can do it

988
Is an unmarked page remarkable

989
Most excuses are poor excuses

990
Breathe in breathe out breathe

991
Let's cure incurable disease

992
Can regular people go postal

993
Life is only a test

994
Yes, the truth sometimes hurts

995
Be free with your favors

996
Don't ever leave your family

997
There is no sure thing

998
Running away is not exercise

999
Wish upon a star tonight

1,000
This is thought one thousand ...

If one thousand aren't enough

I've left some blank pages

For you to add yours

If you feel like sharing:
chaffeekid@aol.com

Thank you all very much.

Made in the USA
Monee, IL
07 November 2022

17302595R00066